My Journey to a Contented Life

*Seven Steps to Help You Heal and Grow to
Create the Life You Want to Live*

Dee Jones

Contents

Published 2025

Printed in the United States of America

ISBN: 978-1-953430-24-3 (pbk)

ISBN: 978-1-953430-23-6 (ebook)

For information, address:

Write and Vibe Publishing at info@writeandvibe.com

This book is dedicated to two of the world's greatest problem solvers that I know – my parents, Warren and Rebecca Hogue. Thank you for a lifetime of love, wisdom, joy, and solutions to so many of my problems. Dad, you taught me the value of hard work and saving money. Mom, you taught me to dream big and love God.

Introduction

"Not that I have already obtained all this, or have already been made perfect, but I press on to take hold of that which Christ Jesus took hold of me. Brothers and sisters, I do not consider myself yet to have taken hold of it. But one thing I do: Forgetting what is behind and straining towards what is ahead, I press on toward the goal to win the prize for which God has called me heavenward in Christ Jesus."
Philippians 3:12-14 (NIV)

This book was born out of a need. The first five years of my marital life was good. During the last 15 years of my marriage to my husband, Devlin, I went through a difficult time. As I look back on our relationship, I believe our foundation began to crack when I thought it was time to have a baby. Devlin and I met at college. We dated several years and broke up our senior year. We each returned to our respective hometowns in Ohio and Pennsylvania. Devlin and I kept in touch after our senior year. We were both looking for jobs and trying to figure out how to be responsible young adults. We got back together as a couple one year after graduation. I refused to move to Pennsylvania, so Devlin agreed to move to Ohio.

Two years later we got married and decided to further our education. We both attended graduate school in the evening while also working full time. Our time was filled with work, classes, and an occasional night out. In hindsight, I would not recommend this kind of lifestyle to any newlyweds.

After graduate school was completed four years later, we exhaled for a year. We purchased our first home and our work-life balance allowed us to relax. In my mind, it was the perfect time to have a baby. We had briefly discussed having a family in our premarital counseling sessions and had both told the pastor that we wanted to have a family. But when I brought it up to Devlin in our fifth year of marriage, he was surprised. Whenever I discussed having a baby, he asked if we could talk about it later. I could not comprehend where his hesitancy came from or if it was going to end. I thought most couples wanted children.

After several conversations, Devlin finally agreed to trying to have a baby. I was elated but after trying for six months with no success, I decided to discuss this matter with Dr. Lee, my OB-GYN. I'd had problems with my menstrual cycle since I was in my twenties and wanted to make sure I was doing the right things to prepare my body for motherhood.

Dr. Lee reviewed my medical records and recommended a change to several medications I was taking at that time. She also ordered several additional tests for me to take over the next four weeks to make sure my reproductive system was functioning properly. Lastly, Dr. Lee provided the names of several specialists for Devlin to see. When I returned home, I told Devlin about my appointment and Dr. Lee's recommendations with a request that he make an appointment as soon as possible.

To provide a sufficient amount of time to visit the specialists and receive our results, Dr. Lee scheduled our follow up appointment in six to eight weeks. I have to make a disclosure; back then, it took a lot longer to get results from medical tests and exams. This was before the online medical systems were created and implemented by medical providers for patients to see their health data online.

At the follow up appointment, Dr. Lee asked if Devlin had made an appointment with one of her referrals. I blurted the first thing that came to my mind, "Of course he did."

But as I sat there staring at Dr. Lee, I was not so sure. I later found out, to my chagrin, that Devlin had *not* made the appointment with a specialist, so Dr. Lee recommended we continue our appointment after Devlin completed his consultation with the specialist. I agreed and left her office feeling hot, angry, and frustrated.

When Devlin got home that evening I asked why he was putting off making the appointment with the specialist. We sat down in the living room. He was so quiet and still; I waited patiently while he collected his thoughts. Devlin finally said he would make the appointment the next day. Due to him acting differently, I asked, "Is something wrong?"

He said, "No."

The silence that night was only the beginning of many more. I began to think over Devlin's behavior since we started talking about having a baby. I also had to ask myself some questions.

Was I forcing him to do something that he did not want to do? I did not think so.

Did I want a child so I could put a check mark on my to do list? No.

Was I trying to fit in with the rest of my family members and friends who were having children? Maybe.

Was this the best way to stop people from asking us when we were going to have a baby? Yes.

And the most important question: did I really want to be a mother? Absolutely.

Devlin kept his word and made an appointment with Dr. Taylor, the specialist, and completed all the tests that Dr. Taylor ordered during their consultation. We had several more doctor appointments after that and received wonderful news; there was a good possibility of us having a baby. I needed to continue to take several medications to help regulate my cycle but otherwise, my health was good.

However, when we met with Dr. Taylor again, he said that based on his review of Devlin's test results, surgery would be required to optimize our chances of having a baby. I was not expecting that kind of news, and neither was Devlin. As Dr. Taylor explained the outpatient procedure, although Devlin and I were sitting within two feet of each other, I felt that he had drifted away to a place where no one could find him. It was a silent ride home.

We had very few questions. I think we both were in shock. Dr. Taylor told us to take our time in thinking over this information and to contact him with any questions.

I did not mention Dr. Taylor's recommendation for three to four weeks. When I got the courage to ask Devlin what he wanted to do, I think I already knew the answer with 85% certainty. He looked at me with those nice, sad, and serious brown eyes and said he was not going to have the surgery. I asked why not. Devlin again stated that he was not interested in having the surgery, but he didn't truly give a reason.

Dr. Taylor had told us during the consultation that without the surgery, the chances of Devlin getting me pregnant would significantly decrease. I thought if I gave Devlin a little more time, he would change his mind. He did not.

After I grudgingly accepted the realization that Devlin did not want to have the surgery, I moved on to other options. I am fairly optimistic and like to think of solutions instead of drowning in despair. My second choice was to have a baby by in vitro fertilization. It would be a costly and invasive process, but I figured it was worth it. Devlin said no.

I then suggested we try adoption. There were so many children that needed love and a home. We were young and healthy with a large family to support us and the child. We could offer the baby all of these things. Devlin said no.

I did not want to hurt Devlin anymore by bringing up the subject of a baby. I thought I could continue our marriage and be content. After all, there were other couples that did not have children and they seemed to have a good life. So, my new focus became enjoying our life as a couple. We traveled, participated in community events and attended a local church regularly. We had a large group of family members and friends who provided us with support and love. But no matter how hard we tried to move on, our lives were not the same.

Devlin changed jobs several times in a five-year period. He became distant, secretive, and did not return calls. I did what I knew to maintain a loving marriage but after all of that effort, we went from being spouses to more like roommates. Although he never said it out loud, I believed that in Devlin's mind if he could not father a child in the most natural of ways, he'd rather not have a child.

I was at my wits end.

I started wondering if anyone had written a book that would help people, particularly Christians, looking for help at a time when they believed their marriages were over, so I went to find one. At bookstores and libraries, I searched the *self-help, improvement,* and all other relevant sections that offered help with marriages. The closest helpful book I found was, "Love Must Be Tough" by James Dobson.

I also discreetly asked people I knew for help. At one point

Devlin and I even met with a counselor but when he stopped attending the meetings, so did I. I know that no one's life is perfect, but I figured there must be a way to get to a better place in my life. I was tired of the strife, anger, stress, and despair. What I really wanted was to be in a good place in my life. I was certain that there were many ways to get there, I just needed a few tips to help me along my way.

About three plus years later, I was at a Bible study in the springtime. One of the hand-outs had the following quote by Toni Morrison at the top of the page, "If there is a book that you want to read, but it has not been written yet, then you must write it."

So began my journey into this project. At first, I thought I was writing this book for people having marital problems, but this book is not just for those struggling in that area. It is a self-help book for all of life's relationship problems.

When I started to write this book, I had several titles in mind. Each title contained some element of what I wanted to convey in this book. I started with "Moving On". Then I went onto "Pressing On". Then I thought the final title would be "Bye Bye to Yesterday". However, something was still missing.

Finally, the right words came together. I wanted people to be able to thrive, not just survive. After you have been hurt, the best thing you can do for yourself is get the help you need to heal and press on ahead. You must be willing to acknowledge your problems and do the work to reach a solution in order to find your path to a better life. There are many ways to get there. This is mine.

I give God the glory for this book. It is my hope that it will fulfill its purpose: to lighten someone's burden.

Peacefully Yours,

DJ

Chapter 1

Stop

"You have six days each week for your ordinary work, but on the seventh day you must stop working...."
Exodus 23:12A (NLT)

Whenever I come up against a difficult problem, my first instinct is normally to run. To run hard. To run fast and to run forever. Sometimes I think that if I keep moving, that is progress. If I keep shifting lanes and getting ahead of other people, I'm in a better place. Right? But the thing about running is that, because I am a human being, I will eventually have to stop.

Life is difficult. If we keep on running, the problems will only increase to the point where they overwhelm our lives. We must stop so that we can focus on what it is we need to do. Stopping helps us not be distracted by other things to the degree that we avoid some of the more complex issues in our lives.

People are designed to try to solve problems. We cannot just let our problems sit there and stare at us; we have to do something about them. Don't we? The thing is, there are some problems that cannot be fixed by human will or determination.

1

When you have been knocked down, sometimes the best thing you can do is stop. To master the art of stopping you must be willing to develop the habits of being still and quiet.

We are told in Psalm 46:10 (A) (NKJV) to, "Be still and know that I am God..."

Some people fear being still. Is it because it feels unproductive? Or maybe we believe no one will miss us if we leave. Perhaps it is because we equate being still with doing nothing or being worthless and thus, if we are doing nothing, then by the world's standards, we are useless. I have heard of the term nervous energy that is used when a person appears to keep moving around or doing something to maintain their sanity.

There is a positive side to keeping busy, it's when you are productive and not hurting yourself and others. But if being busy is used as a tool to avoid addressing the major issues in our lives, we are not helping ourselves or anyone else.

Being still is:

1. As much of an emotional act as a physical act.
2. As much of a spiritual act as a physical act.
3. As much of a mental act as a physical act.

For me, being still is more than stopping your physical body from engaging in some kind of activity. It means that you are allowing your heart, mind, body, and soul to shut down their functions at their everyday hectic pace.

For others, being still means different things. A friend of mine, April, told me a story about a time in her life when she had to make some difficult decisions. She'd become disenchanted with her church life and didn't know what to do so she took a break. She did not attend any church for almost a year. However, April still enjoyed her time with God and read her Bible. It was in this season of her leave from church that she gained a new perspective as to what she needed to do in her life. Many people did not understand why she stayed away from the church for a year, but it was the right thing for *her* to do. April had to stop going to church to re-establish her understanding of what God's purpose was for her life.

What happens if you keep running away from your problems? You will still be able to go on with your life, but it will not be in the most beneficial way. That green elephant sitting in the middle of your bed is not going to leave anytime soon. Problems do not go away and situations are not resolved until we become intentional about addressing them, one at a time. Just as proper maintenance is required for a car to run, it is the same with our bodies, minds, and souls. If you fail to get your car's oil changed at the proper time, refuse to take your car to a mechanic when one of the warning signals appears on your dashboard, or you hear your car making a strange noise and still do nothing, you will eventually find yourself sitting in a vehicle that has broken down.

Stopping is not just a luxury; it is a necessity. We live in a very fast paced and hurried world. Each day, new and different demands come our way. When you become weary by the everyday events in your life, you cannot function properly in addressing those demands. You can also become physically, mentally, emotionally, and spiritually ill.

One evening I was watching a program on the local PBS station that was about a complex organ – the brain. Several doctors were on the program and one of them mentioned how we all need to slow down. He believed that we have so many neurological problems because of the increase in multi-tasking. Multi-tasking is like having too many plugs in one outlet. Eventually the breaker trips or an electrical fire starts. The brain is the same way. It can get overloaded with too much data, information, and emotions that continuously flow through it twenty-four hours a day.

The doctor further stated that our brain was designed to handle one thing at a time. That bears repeating. Our brain is designed to handle one thing at a time. So when I am cooking, talking on the phone, and thinking about next week's board meeting, I am really doing a disservice to my brain and in turn, myself.

It is time to stop the madness! It may take a while, but we need to try to develop the discipline of thinking about one thing at a time. It may seem impossible in our twenty-first century world, but give it a try. What do you have to lose besides stress, anxiety, fear, insomnia, and other things which are harmful to your health?

It takes courage to be still. Sallie was an acquaintance and a former local politician in my community. She served in many different positions as she rose up the ranks to a top-level position in her career, but when Sallie made it to the top, she was reminded of how cutthroat the political world could be. People she was good friends with turned into enemies and her former allies became people she had to keep an eye on just to make sure they didn't stab her in the back. In politics, there are no permanent friends and no permanent enemies. Some people in her community believed that it was time for a change.

Because of all of that, Sallie did not win her seat when she ran for re-election. She was disappointed because she still believed she had a great deal to offer her constituents. Sallie was worn out, mad, and frustrated. She decided to take a long break and at one point, she spent a few weeks in bed. Her husband, Paul, would check on her and ask what she planned to do that day. Sallie's response was always that she planned to do nothing because she needed to stop and just be still. Then, maybe tomorrow, she'd decide what to do. Sallie never returned to the world of politics. Instead, she applied her skills and talents to several businesses.

She has no regrets.

Did you know that God's Word, the Bible, says a lot about stopping and resting? In the book of Leviticus 23:21, 23-24A (NLT), you will find these words:

"That same day will be proclaimed an official day for holy assembly, a day on which you do no ordinary work. This is a permanent law for you, and it must be observed from generation to generation, wherever you live...The Lord said to Moses, "Give the following instructions to the people of Israel. On the first day of the appointed month in early autumn you are to observe a day of complete rest...""

God knows us. He knows how we can fill our time with things that do not matter, which is why He was very clear when He told Moses the instructions for the Israelites concerning the appointed festivals. God did not want the Israelites to have a good time and go home. He wanted the Israelites to stop and rest so that they would be able to focus on and understand the meaning of these festivals.

It is difficult to understand something if you are overwhelmed or exhausted. When you stop, you are giving yourself time to be still so that you can be ready for the road ahead. If you don't stop, you will miss out on so many things that you need to learn in order to grow in a way that honors God and will be a blessing to you, your family, and the world.

The way that I stop myself is probably not typical of most people. I turn off the television and refuse to answer the phone. Then, I sit or lay in a comfortable position and breathe in and out. I imagine myself in a peaceful place. I know that I am getting to that peaceful place when I can hear myself breathing. Thoughts, as they often tend to, will try to intrude and distract me. It is through much hard work and discipline that I have been able to keep myself still and not start to do things.

Most mornings, my mother sits in her recliner and turns on her television to watch a channel that plays relaxing music with beautiful nature scenes appearing on the screen throughout the program. She finds this practice to be a soothing way to begin her day. Another way to be still is by enjoying nature. You may want to sit in your backyard and listen to everything that is going on around you or take a slow and gentle hike in a nearby park. If you are fortunate like me, you can go to the lakeshore. Watching the waves coming and going while the sun is rising or setting can be comforting. Listening to music that brings you into a tranquil space can also be helpful. A friend of mine sits by his fire pit at the end of the day. Breathing in the cool night air and watching the golden ambers brings a calmness to his soul.

Being still is considered boring by some. Our society does not embrace being still. I've heard some people ask others who are sitting quietly if they are doing some kind of religious thing, like meditating or praying. Most of us would rather do anything to keep from being bored. If boredom is for losers, should we say the same thing about being still? Boredom tends to lead to other behaviors such as frustration, impatience, irritability, and negativity.

There are several benefits from being still. Stillness helps us to be intentional about slowing ourselves down. Stillness allows us to regulate our breathing and lower our heart rates. By being still, we give ourselves the opportunity to stay in this present moment in time and experience a sense of peace and possibly joy. It is in my time of stillness that I obtain a better understanding of the human condition.

It is usually impossible to be still without being quiet. Some people are uncomfortable with silence. We live in a world filled with music, voices, noises, and all kinds of sounds twenty-four hours a day. It is the norm to have some kind of sound going on around us. Sometimes we use sounds to fill a void in our lives. Perhaps it is due to loneliness, anxiety, or depression.

When we find that we need silence, it is unrealistic to ask family members to be silent at the same time. But we could, like in the classroom, schedule some quiet time in our homes. I remember visiting a relative in another state. He lived in a small town with no sidewalks on his street. My first evening I don't recall hearing any cars driving up and down the street or the sound of the neighbor's conversation, music, or television. I could hear the leaves blowing on the trees and the sound of birds chirping nearby. It was a lovely way to end the first day of my visit. I slept through the night and woke up refreshed and ready for a magnificent day. It may seem impossible to find a quiet moment, but those moments exist. You must be intentional about making it happen.

One of the best ways I have gotten to know myself better is by being still. I believe that most people don't know themselves because they have never taken the time to be still. Our culture has a great influence on why we have trouble being still. Some people find very little value in being still. A general perception is if you are doing nothing, you will be left behind. We applaud those who work twelve-to-sixteen-hour shifts per day. We envy people who go out to various social events four to five times a week. Others enjoy looking at their busy schedules, not even realizing that they did not make time for their family or meals. In America, we have many clever catch phrases about making your job your number one priority, such as if you snooze you lose, the early bird catches the worm, burning the midnight oil, and carpe diem.

If a celebrity or influencer mentioned they were going to start being intentionally still, so many of their millions of followers would join them. Stillness, like eating more fruits and vegetables, is not a habit you may like at first, but once you get started, you will realize the benefits and reap the rewards.

How well do you know yourself? I sometimes ask people what I believe to be very simple questions. What do you like to do for fun? What is one of your happiest memories? Who is someone outside of your family that you respect or admire?

Can you answer those questions? If not today, maybe in time you will be able to answer them as you get to know yourself on a deeper level.

When you stop, you are giving yourself a gift. You are, in essence, saying to yourself, "I am so important to this world that I need to take time for myself."

But the gift is not what you think it is. Your problems won't just disappear. People won't simply become loving human beings. The world will keep spinning. What *will* happen when you stop is that you will receive the gift of opportunity. The opportunity to get to know yourself. Then, you can begin the journey of healing your body, heart, mind, and soul.

After I stopped trying to make my marriage work my life got better. Devlin and I decided to separate in order to give ourselves a much-needed break from our relationship. So, do not be afraid to stop for a little while. You may miss a good joke, an episode of your favorite series, or the next hit song, but you will also gain the privilege of getting to know yourself in a whole new way. Isn't it worth it? Aren't you worth it? Absolutely!

Exercise 1

Be intentional about finding some quiet time to be still for a while. Turn off the television, your cell phone, and mute anything else that could be distracting. If you have young children you may need to plan your quiet time around their schedule, such as while they are taking a nap or at school. Maybe they can visit a relative or friend's house for an hour or two.

You can also ask those in your home to do something quietly for a while, such as read several chapters of a book or use their earbuds if they are planning on utilizing their laptops, tablets, or cellphones at the same time.

Now have a seat or lay down in a comfortable place. Imagine yourself putting each of your thoughts, feelings, and problems in their own little boat and pushing them out into the sea. Or gather all of them up and place them inside of your luggage, making sure not to leave any of them out. Once they're all in, don't peek inside your luggage to see what those problems are doing; they will be fine on their own for a little while. Just leave them alone.

Now, be still. Can you feel your heart beating? Try to relax all of your muscles from your head to your feet. Let your breathing become slower as you gently exhale. You may need more than a few minutes in order to develop the discipline of stopping and being still; it depends on what is reasonable for your situation. By the way, it is okay if you find yourself falling asleep. Sleep is a form of being still.

You will never have or find the time to be still, you need to make the time. Please don't use your family, job, friends, or church as an excuse as to why you can't make the time. You must do this for you. I suggest you pull out that busy planner and write down a time to stop.

You know how you schedule playdates, doctor's appointments, and vacation time? Each week you need to look over your life and your schedule to plan a time to stop. I suggest you start with once a week for thirty minutes. Like any good habit, it will take some time to develop. After you have stopped yourself, you are now ready to move to another step in your journey.

Chapter 2

Pray

"Pray without ceasing."
I Thessalonians 5:17 (NKJV)

When you don't know what to do, do nothing. That was step one. Now that you have removed most of the distractions, it's time to pray. We are told in Philippians 4:6-7 (NKJV) to, "Be anxious for nothing, but in everything by prayer and supplication with thanksgiving, let your request be made known to God; and the peace of God, which surpasses all understanding, will guard your hearts and minds through Christ Jesus."

In order to receive clear direction for what to do next, you must be very careful to whom you go to for advice.

After I separated from Devlin, I found myself in a weird place. I wasn't exactly a wife anymore. But I was not single. I could not call on my husband to fix the toilet and at the same time, I could not meet a male friend for dinner after work. Being in this title-less space made me feel uncomfortable and lost. During this time, I received a lot of advice from family members and friends. I was somewhat surprised at their suggestions. One family member wanted me to meet one of his friends. Another friend felt it was all right for me to go out and date someone else since my spouse had moved out of our house. My problem with their suggestions was that I was still in a covenant relationship that included God, me, and my spouse. God had not released me from the marriage so I could not just move on.

My family and friends were not trying to hurt me, they were trying to help me move on with my life. I understood and appreciated their efforts. I knew that dating and getting involved in a new relationship with another man was not the right thing for me to do when my life was such a mess. How did I know? For one thing, I saw what happened to other people who tried to date while married. Doing so made a messy situation all the more confusing and heartbreaking. It was also due to my relationship with God.

This in-between space was frustrating and lonely. The first few months after our separation, I could not believe I was in this situation. I had thought that since I was a good, decent, and caring person, that things should have worked out for me. When I thought about all the time I invested in my marriage, I got so angry. There was so much emotional pain that it felt like it was radiating from everywhere at the same time.

It's like, if you fall off a bike, scrape your elbow, bruise your knee, and twist your ankle, you don't know which area is hurting the most because you feel such a deep and intense throbbing pain from all of those areas. Unfortunately, this kind of pain cannot be dealt with by taking an aspirin or covering it with a Band-Aid.

When I could not hold things in anymore, I vented to my family, friends, and close church members. If I saw someone who looked like Devlin, I clinched my teeth and glared at him. If anyone mentioned his name, I had to count to ten, if not twenty, before I responded. But through it all, God was gracious enough to give me a sense of peace to keep me from going over the edge of the cliff.

In all my troubles, God showed me which way to go, and He will do the same for you. Only God can give you the best directions. God *does* answer prayers. He may not answer them in your timeframe or provide the answer you want to hear, but He will answer your prayers. You don't have to worry about praying a specific prayer or doing the "right" thing. There is no standard way to pray, so do what works best for you.

Some people pray in the morning. Others pray in the evening. Some people pray on their knees and others pray while lying on the floor. You can pray in your bedroom, a parked car, or while riding on a bus. Some people pray out loud. Others pray quietly. God is not into a specific technique. He's into you.

Prayer requires time and attention. It is a most serious and wonderful endeavor. Just think, God is available to each of us twenty-four hours a day, seven days a week. I encourage you to develop the habit of praying. God does not mind if you customize your prayer in a way that works best for you; He is just delighted to hear from you.

When you pray, you can tell God anything and everything. When I realized that my marriage was falling apart and we still lived together, my initial prayers the first few years went something like this: *Dear Lord, I know that things are not right in my marriage. I know that we both have done some destructive things that have weakened our marital bond. Please help us. We need your guidance and wisdom to see us through this storm. We will not make it without You. I thank You for listening and being by my side. In the name of Jesus. Amen.*

Then, after my husband refused to continue to attend marital counseling sessions, my prayers turned into the direction of miracles, so I prayed: *Dear Heavenly Father, I believe that*

You parted the Red Sea, allowed Sarah to give birth to a baby boy in her 90s and gave a blind man sight. If You can do those things, You can surely save my marriage. Please change both of our hearts so that we can rekindle the love we had for one another and be reconciled in our marriage. I know You can do all things. In the name of Jesus. Amen.

During this time, I was more discerning of whom I sought counseling from day by day. One of my friends, who is a minister, gave me some sound advice. Reverend Green said that when I had felt that I had done all that I could do as a godly wife to save my marriage, then it was time to ask the Lord what the next step was. I believed I had three options. I could ask Devlin to move out. We could live in the same house as housemates. Or I could move out.

My prayer at this turning point of my marriage was somewhat like this: *Dear Lord, please give me a sense of peace if I have done all that I can do to save my marriage. My heart is broken, and I am weary of trying to do the right things. Help me to stop holding onto something that I need to let go. Show me how to be a woman of grace and dignity as I navigate the days ahead. No matter what I want or think I deserve, Lord, Your will be done in my life. Thank You for Your love. In the name of Jesus. Amen.*

I had asked Devlin too many times what he wanted to do regarding his plans for moving out of the house, but he never gave me a clear answer. I asked him to move out several times a month, but he always said no. One morning he gave what I'm sure he thought was a clever response. After asking him for the umpteenth time what was the problem with him moving out, he looked at me and said, "You just might have a good life without me."

It was then that I decided to move out of our house. As I looked to my future, I continued to pray. After a few weeks of apartment hunting, I felt like I had given up enough of my time and energy, so I decided to stay in our house. We were not getting any younger. After fifteen plus years of marriage, I knew it was time to get serious about ending our marriage. Our last conversation at our house was not a long one. I looked Devlin in the eyes and told him that I had been a good wife to him and he knew what he needed to do.

I asked Devlin for the final time to move out of our house that weekend. I went away for the weekend to give him some space. When I returned on Sunday afternoon, Devlin's SUV was not in the garage. As I was opening the side door to enter my house, I felt like a weight had been lifted off of my shoulders. The house seemed brighter and the air fresher. I made my way upstairs to the bedroom and checked Devlin's closet. It was empty. There weren't any suits, shirts, ties, or shoes. His underwear, socks, and pajamas had been removed from the drawers. Most of the things that Devlin owned were gone.

Over the next few weeks my constant prayer was: *Dear Lord, please do not let me become an angry and bitter woman. You have brought me too far and continued to bless my life during this terrible time. I need You and I don't want to run You away. Please show me how to be a loving and faithful daughter. Thank You for all that You do for me. I love You Lord. In the name of Jesus. Amen.*

Someone once said that prayer is a conversation with God. As you know, a conversation usually includes two or more persons in communication with one another. When I first began to pray, I would use what I defined as my holy soft voice. It was not my everyday voice, but a soft and whispery tone I made up, which I thought would help my prayers. I would then proceed to tell God what I needed or wanted, who was bothering me or why it was not my fault when I did something wrong. I was treating God like a genie in a bottle.

After I gave God my wish list for the day, I would go on my merry way. For many years, I only prayed when I needed something. I did not realize I was using God. Can you imagine a relationship where someone contacted you only in those times when they needed something from you? That is not a healthy, enjoyable, or productive relationship. Prayer does not mean you only tell God what is on your heart, mind, and soul, but you also wait to hear what God has to say to you.

My life changed when I got serious about God. I discovered a commonality among the people in my life who were kind, wise, honest, persistent, and mature. Most, if not all of them had a relationship with God. I wanted to get there but in order to do so, I needed a deeper relationship with God. I wanted to know Him. There was no way I was going to know God if I never took the time to be still and listen to Him. God had brought me through so much in my life. I longed for a closer walk with Him.

My prayer life became more meaningful after I started intentionally spending quiet moments with God through reading the Bible and being around other mature Christians. My desire to get to know God better led to me being more open and transparent with Him and others.

Prayer is not about perfection, proper diction, or memorizing scriptures. Prayer is about sincere and heartfelt moments with God. When my day gets busy and I forget to pray, I actually miss my time with God. My day is not the same when He is not a part of it. I am still a work in progress when it comes to praying. My prayers are not perfect, but God knows they come from my heart.

Sometimes God answers me through His Word, the Bible. I do not think it is a coincidence when I am led to read a scripture or devotion which directly addresses the problem I am dealing with in my life. Other times God answers me through people. Several years ago, I was in a grocery store. I am not a shopper. I get in and I get out as quickly as I can. As I was pushing my cart down an aisle, I could see a lady looking over at me, just glancing over her shoulder. I was not having a very good day and I'm sure my attire and hairstyle reflected my feelings of despair and fatigue. After I had gotten everything on my list I made my way to the cashier. There were a few people in front of me. The strange thing was that the same lady who glanced at me earlier in the store was in front of me. I'll call her Angel.

Angel glanced at me a few times as she took her groceries out of her cart and placed them on the conveyor belt. I began to get annoyed. I mean, I know I'm not a beauty queen, but really? I gave her my best, "What is your problem?" look.

Finally, it was my turn to put my items on the conveyor belt and pay for my groceries. As I pushed my cart towards the exit, there was Angel. She looked like she was waiting for me. Why else would she still be hanging around the exit area? Angel must have seen the irritation on my face. She asked if she could speak to me for a minute. I wondered if this was some kind of scam or a new way to tell people about her church or religion. I nodded my head.

We stepped aside and Angel said that she did not want to do this.

"Do what?" I asked.

She said that she was not crazy and that God told her to tell me that everything was going to be all right. Angel then explained she had been prompted before to give someone a message from God, but she refused because she did not want people to think that she was crazy. Angel asked me if any of this made sense.

I said, "Yes, I've been waiting on an answer about some things going on in my life. Your statement let me know I was on the right path."

Angel gave me a self-conscious half smile and waved goodbye. God uses people and things as He will. Other times, God performs a miracle by placing His answer right before me. When I was in a particularly painful and dark place in my life, I prayed and experienced a comfort like I had never known before. Then I remembered the following scripture:

"In my distress, I called upon the Lord and cried to my God; He heard my voice from His temple; and my cry entered His ears...He bowed the heavens also, and came down with darkness under His feet...He sent from above, He took me; He drew me out of many waters. He delivered me from my strong enemy. From those who hated me; for they were too strong for me. They confronted me in the day of my calamity, but the Lord was my support. He also brought me out into a broad place; He delivered me because He delighted in me."

II Samuel 22:7, 10, 17-20 (NKJV)

Amazing things happen when we pray. It is one of the most powerful gifts I use each day of my life. There were many times when I simply did not understand why my marriage was so painful. One evening I was crying out to God asking Him what I had done wrong in my marriage. It was a long sorrowful prayer time. The tears ran down my eyes, cheeks, and jaw as they landed on my top, one drop at a time. When I thought I could cry no more, I heard a still soft voice say to me, "You have done nothing wrong. You have nothing to be ashamed of."

Hearing those words was another turning point in my life. Sometimes guilt and fear can distort your vision to a point where you feel vulnerable and question your self-worth daily. When God got a grip on me and pulled me back into His truth, I knew I was going to be alright.

Here's the thing about prayer, once you start to increase your prayer time, you will naturally want to know more about God. One of the best ways to know God better is by reading and meditating on His Word. It is a treasure and its value is greatly underestimated. The Bible is not just a book of good reading material, it is God's Word, which is available to anyone and everyone whosoever chooses to learn more about Him. My heart aches at the number of Bibles that sit on coffee tables unopened, collecting dust on a bookshelf or those that are stored in a box in the attic or basement. I heard a statistic last year that astonished me. In one poll, the results indicated that about ten percent of people who call themselves Christians read their Bible every day. The Psalmist told us: "Your word is a lamp to my feet and a light to my path." Psalm 119:105 (NKJV).

If you want to see the path that you should be on, get into God's Word. Another way you can get to know God is through fellowship with other mature Christians. Notice that I said mature Christian. Some people may call themselves a Christian, but they do not have a growing relationship with God. A mature Christian is one who prays, reads their Bible and lives their life in a way that honors God. This person will also be a blessing to those around them.

Having someone to pray with you and for you is a wonderful gift. Sometimes I have not been able to pray for myself due to illness, heartache or stubbornness. It is during those times that I have had other people pray for me. My mother called me once. She was so excited and could not wait to share her good news. On one of the coldest weekdays in February, her furnace decided to start making a strange noise. No heat was coming out from furnace. It would come on, make a thumping noise, and turn off. All day long she heard the same tune. Mom called Mr. Fuller, a furnace repairman, on Friday. He came the next morning and was able to diagnose and repair the furnace within two hours. Mom gave him a check to pay for his services.

The house was warm and comfortable by the time we spoke that evening. Mom stated how happy she was to have her heat on again. She said that Mr. Fuller asked her a very interesting question as he was putting away his tools. He wanted to know if it was okay to pray with the family before he left. Of course, Mom said yes. He asked if anything in particular was bothering Mom, and she mentioned that the arthritis in her hands had been giving her some pain for a long time. Several relatives were visiting my mother this day. Mr. Fulller requested that everyone come together in a circle and hold hands. He said a beautiful prayer for Mom and our family. After finishing, Mom thanked Mr. Fuller for everything, especially the prayer. She said she had never experienced anything like that before – a repairman praying for her!

As you begin your prayer life, do not worry about your words. Just imagine yourself talking to a friend, to your best friend, to someone who knows all about you and will love you forever. If you pray in this way, in time, your prayer life will be as natural to you as breathing-something you do without even thinking about each day of your life. As I Thessalonians 5:17 says, "pray without ceasing" until your answer comes from God.

Exercise 2

Design a prayer environment that works for you. I tend to lean towards a time of quietness where I am either kneeling on the floor near my bed or sitting in a comfortable chair. Sometimes I sit on my sofa where I can feel the sunshine on my face from the front window. You may wish to have some soothing instrumental music softly playing in the background. You can also light a few candles or incense to help relax your body and mind. Take a few moments to inhale and exhale. Try to pick a favorite spot where you feel safe and relaxed.

If you are not sure how to pray, first ask God to help you. Do you have a good friend who you talk to at least once a week? Prayer is like talking to your best friend. Take your time. No one is going to give you a grade or expect perfect diction. The Bible is filled with some sincere and beautiful prayers. One of the most popular chapters of the Bible is the 23rd Psalm. If you have not read the 23rd Psalm, this might be a place to start your prayer time. You might think about attending a local church service. You will find that it is not just the minister, but other members of the church who also participate in a time of prayer.

Some of us are fortunate to have a praying mother, father, grandparent, other relative or friend whose words touch our hearts and souls.

There are also several apps and books on the subject. The internet, cable, and streaming services provide numerous resources on prayer. You will notice that there is no one particular way to pray. You may want to write down a few things to help you to remember what you want to include in your prayers. Get in the habit of having pen and paper nearby. It is okay to jot things down and then go back to your prayer time. We are human beings, not robots. Some people write out their prayers.

The important thing to remember is that this is a time to find a quiet and comfortable place to enjoy your time with God. However, and wherever you pray, be transparent (willing to reveal all the good, bad, and ugly things about yourself), and available to hear what God has to say to you. When God speaks, listen ever so carefully to His instructions and advice. If you do not hear from God immediately, don't give up. Some of the best things in life take time. This is so true when it comes to developing your prayer time with God.

Chapter 3

Forgive

Jesus prayed, "Father forgive them; they don't know what they are doing."
Luke 23:34A (MSG)

Have you ever been hurt? Did someone you love betray you? Were you ever passed over for a promotion, not because you were unqualified, but because the person selected had a personal or political connection to those in power? That sense of bitterness, anger, and self-righteous indignation can eat away at your heart, mind, body, and soul if you are still holding on to these feelings. It can literally make you sick. Forgiveness is a beautiful concept. It may appear to be an easy action to do occasionally, but putting it into practice on a daily basis can be difficult.

I attended a seminar on forgiveness several years ago. One of the presenters was a psychologist who explained how unforgiveness affects your thoughts in a negative way. Unforgiveness can lead to harboring bad feelings, not only for the person who you believed committed the unforgivable act, but it also spreads those same bad feelings towards others. Guilty by association, some would say. Another presenter explained how unforgiveness can lead to stress. We all should know what stress can do to us. It affects the body in many ways and can cause all kinds of ailments to manifest physically and mentally. We can develop heart problems from high blood pressure or obesity from overeating. Unforgiveness will affect every area of your life, including your relationships, your home, work, church, and self. It is a deadly disease that needs to be stopped before it destroys you.

Another sentiment that was emphasized at the seminar by a pastor was that forgiveness is not optional. If you love God, you must forgive others. The Disciple's Prayer can be found in the Bible, in the book of Matthew 6:8-13. Many Christians are familiar with these verses, however; it is very important to keep reading through to the next two verses to fully understand just how serious God is about forgiveness. "In prayer there is a connection between what God does and what you do. You can't get forgiveness from God for instance, without also forgiving others. If you refuse to do your part, you cut yourself off from God's part." Matthew 6:14-15 (MSG).

This scripture makes it all very simple. If you do not forgive others, God is not going to forgive you. It won't be easy. But it is the right thing to do.

Forgiveness is a divine habit to incorporate into your life. How does one forgive another? One of the first things I do is to pray and ask God for His help. We live in a cruel, evil, and selfish world. People do unimaginable things to each other every day. The only way not to go insane is to ask for help. It took me several years to get to a place where I finally stopped blaming Devlin for everything that went wrong in our marriage. It was then that I was able to see things a lot clearer. Blame can cloud your vision and hinder you from working on the healing you deserve. When I set the blame aside, I was able to see myself and the role I played in the erosion of the foundation of our marriage.

Part of my problem was me. I like to quantify things. In my mind, if I am forty-nine percent or less at fault, then the other person should shoulder all, if not most, of the blame. For many years, in my heart, I believed Devlin was the cause of all of our marital problems. An immature mindset like this will keep you from growing into a mature and responsible adult. Several years after meeting with the specialists, I was still praying about our marriage and my life. During one of these prayer times, the Lord told me that I had to forgive Devlin from my heart. As if that were not enough, I also needed to ask for his forgiveness.

What? Why should I have to ask for his forgiveness? Even though I knew I could not get forgiveness from God until I forgave Devlin, this was still a humongous and bitter pill to swallow. I felt raw and exposed, like someone was peeling my skin from my body. I was in an uncomfortable place for several months. The Lord had to continue to work with me until I could sincerely forgive Devlin from my heart. For only then, would I be able to extend a true apology.

As I reflected on the life that Devlin and I shared, I recalled the smart and intense young man that I met at college who had a quirky sense of humor; the new husband who tried to make me happy in so many ways and the helpmate who was a steady shoulder to lean on for me and my family during one of the worst times in our lives. That was the Devlin that I grew to love, respect, and cherish. Remembering the good things about Devlin and the great times we had together as a couple made apologizing so much easier.

During the last two to three years of living together, Devlin and I would have our *what are we going to do about our marriage* conversations. It was mainly at my request; most times he remained silent. It was during one of these sessions that I told Devlin that I was sorry for all the ways that I had failed him and us. The apology was not as painful or difficult as I thought it would be for me. I don't remember how he responded to my apology, but I do remember that I felt good about myself and could look at Devlin with compassion and hope afterwards.

I also look to other people for examples on how they have handled terrible events. Corrie Ten Boom was an evangelist and member of the Dutch Reformed Church in the Netherlands. After World War II, she and her family hid Jews fleeing from Germany. In February 1944, the German secret service received a tip from someone and raided the Ten Boom home. Thirty people were arrested, including Corrie, her father, and sister, Betsie. Mr. Ten Boom died 10 days after being arrested.

In September 1944, Corrie and Betsie were placed in a concentration camp in Germany. Corrie was able to smuggle her Bible into the concentration camp. They lived in a building with 700 other prisoners that was built to hold 200. The women prisoners were subjected to strip searches in front of male guards. The male prisoners were lined up, shot, and killed in an area behind the camp. Many times, the prisoners were taken out of the building on the premise that they were going to get a shower. Instead, they were placed in a room filled with poisonous gas and killed.

Betsie was beaten often for being a slow worker and eventually starved to death. Her body was added to many others waiting to be dumped into a large burial hole. Corrie said her sister had a smile on her face when she died in December 1944. Corrie was released a short time later from the Ravensbruck Concentration Camp and she returned to her home in the Netherlands where she continued to preach God's word. For the remainder of her life, she traveled across the world preaching the goodness of God and telling her story.

During one of her lectures, Corrie saw one of the prison guards who had been very cruel to Betsie. After her speech, the guard walked up to her and told her he was now a Christian. He asked Corrie to forgive him for all the terrible things he had done. At first, she found that hard to do, but with God's help, she forgave him. She knew she would not be able to move on with her life until she forgave her former oppressor.

Another instance of forgiveness came about as I was watching an evening news program several years ago. There was a story about a young lady from the United States who traveled to a country in Africa with a charitable organization. The organization's focus was to help make life better for the communities in the rural areas. The young lady had left her family and friends to travel thousands of miles away to be used for something good. She was in her twenties with all of the lovely things in life in front of her, but she was killed while serving others. It seemed so senseless. Why would a person kill someone who was trying to help make the quality of life better for others?

Her parents were understandably brokenhearted, but they remembered their daughter's passion for her cause and how much she enjoyed helping the people in that African community. The parents knew that most of the people in that community were grateful for their daughter and the organization's help. They also realized that the people in the community were grieved by the death of someone who had made such a positive difference in their lives.

The parents decided to go visit the town where their daughter had been killed. They were not going there to kill anyone in revenge for their daughter's death. It was not their intention to mourn over the place where she had died. They were traveling there to experience the passion their daughter had for serving others, so they could see that their daughter's life had not been lived in vain. While in the country, they met and talked with the people who had spent time with their daughter. They knew that they could not help themselves or anyone else until they forgave the people who had killed their daughter. So that's what they did.

In a book given to me by my mother, there was a quote by pastor and writer, Max Lucado, that has been an anchor for me when I try to set sail on the "ship of unforgiveness." Pastor Lucado said, "You will never forgive anyone more than God has already forgiven you."

This is a fact. The worst thing that anyone has ever done to me does not compare to the things I do to God. I remember a time when I begged God to get me out of a bad situation. Patti was one of my good friends in high school. Patti and I had been asked out on a double date by two young men, Naaman and Joab, students from a nearby high school. We had known them for a few months.

We were told that we were going to their friend's party in a nearby town. I wanted to go out with Joab so badly that we lied to our guardians about our evening plans. After Naaman and Joab picked us up, Joab and I sat in the back seat while Patti sat up front with Naaman, who was the driver. We were so busy laughing and talking in the car that we did not notice the time nor where we were going. They drove us to a place that was an hour from my house.

When we got out the car, I did not see any cars in the driveway, hear any music coming from the house, or see people hanging out on the front porch. I knew I was in trouble. Naaman told us that we were stopping by a friend's house for a little while. As we slowly walked up the stairs to the front door of the dimly lit and quiet house, I wanted to cry.

This was before the invention of the cell phone, Lyft, or Uber, and since Naaman was the driver, we were stuck. I was so scared I was going to be raped or murdered. I promised God that if I got out of that situation, I'd never do anything that stupid again.

Naaman unlocked the door and turned on a light as we all went inside. They asked if we wanted something to drink as they guided us to our seats in the living room. We both said no. Patti and I were sitting too far apart to talk to one another. I wondered what she was thinking. I wondered if anybody would ever find us. I felt like a complete fool.

After several pathetic attempts to kiss me, I told Joab this was not right. I also heard Patti talking to Naaman in a loud and authoritative voice, stating he needed to take us home since we were not going to a party. Patti had a way of looking at you and letting you know she was not the one to mess with and I was very grateful for that then.

Naaman and Joab looked at us and after a few excruciating seconds of silence, agreed to take us home. It was an awkward and tense ride home. This was not how I expected my date with Joab to end. I could not look at him. When Naaman pulled into the driveway, we got out his car and did not look back. I don't know what I would have done if Patti had not been with me. I was so grateful she got us out of there and back home safely. It took some time for me to forgive myself for getting into that situation, but God forgave me and helped me get my act together.

You cannot press forward in your life without forgiving others. This reminds me of situation that I had to come to terms with twenty plus years ago. I had a co-worker, Ethan, who asked me if I would write a letter of recommendation focusing on his duties with the company. I assumed this letter was for another job opportunity, so I typed it up and gave it back within a week.

I later found out that the letter was not for a better job opportunity, but was given to his attorney in support of a pending case where he was the defendant. I was very angry with Ethan for not telling me the truth. I decided that day that I

Dee Jones

would not write another letter of recommendation for anyone. No exceptions.

For several years, whenever someone asked me to write a letter of recommendation, I thought of Ethan and declined. Unforgiveness led me to miss out on helping some very deserving individuals in their careers. What a shame. I finally came to my senses and started writing letters of recommendations after I got a clear understanding of what the letter would be used for each and every time.

Unforgiveness can lead to us becoming some very petty, pious, and lonely individuals. It can also lead to us missing out on some blessings. A few years ago, when my then fiancé, James, and I were planning our wedding, we needed to make some major decisions within a six-month time frame. One of the tasks was the selection of a photographer. We had several referrals whose prices were reasonable.

My niece, Faith, asked if I had thought about using her cousin, Kyle. Kyle's uncle, Adam, had done something that hurt my family terribly thirty years ago. I did not know if my family would want to be around anyone related to Adam, so I spoke with my family about my concerns. They said it would be fine if we chose Kyle as our photographer.

We met with Kyle and discussed what we were looking for in terms of the photographs to be taken in the various locations, events we wanted to be photographed during our wedding day, and the amount of time we needed him for our special day. Kyle was available and gave us a good quote, so we decided to use Kyle as our wedding photographer. He was a true professional who took a great set of photographs.

I spoke with Kyle a few weeks after our wedding. He said something that surprised me. Kyle told me that he really missed my sister, Olivia. Olivia had been married to his uncle Adam for more than 18 years at the time of her death. After Olivia's death, our family had minimal contact with Adam's family. Kyle shared several stories about his personal relationship with Olivia and how much she meant to him. In all of the pain and despair these last thirty years, I forgot that other people were hurting just like my family. I thanked Kyle for sharing his memories with me. I am glad that my family chose to forgive and continue to heal, rather than harbor unforgiving and angry feelings at someone who was also in pain.

Sometimes we may need to forgive someone several times. I had a relative, Lena, whose actions had led to a great deal of frustration and emotional pain in my life and my other family members. Although I tried to reconcile our differences several times, our relationship was not a healthy one.

It is hard to forgive someone who refuses to acknowledge the hurt they have caused others. It got to the point that when I saw her face or heard her voice, my pulse rate increased, my body tensed up, and I braced myself for the foolish things she was going to say or do. Being around her caused me unnecessary stress so I started to either limit, or stop attending certain family events.

But then I realized I was giving Lena power over my life, so I prayed for her. I had to forgive Lena so I could move on with my life. In taking my power back, I realized that I had a choice. I could let Lena dominate the event with her words and actions, or I could be a positive change agent and bring love, light, and laughter into that space. Our family gatherings are much more enjoyable these days. When Lena cannot take over the flow of the conversation or event, she is either quiet or leaves the room. Forgiveness has allowed me to accept Lena for the person she is, but not allow her behavior to ruin a good time.

We have all done things that we regret. Perhaps you have lied to a parent or spouse. Maybe, for a variety of reasons, you decided to have an abortion. Sometimes we feel like we have no other choice, but to cheat on a test or pay someone to write an essay for us. Whatever the circumstance, you must also learn to forgive yourself. When I first thought about the incident with Naaman and Joab, I felt ashamed and foolish. Then I remembered that every experience in my life was a learning lesson.

What did I learn from that incident? To tell the truth, especially to the people who love and care about you. If you have to lie, maybe you need to think twice before proceeding with your plans. Secondly, always have a backup plan to get home. It might be embarrassing to get someone out of bed to pick you up after midnight, but make the call anyway. It could save your life or keep you from harm. Thirdly, be careful of the people who you let into your life. The young men seemed decent, but their words and actions proved that they were not men of integrity.

Lighten your load. Forgive someone, including yourself today. It is the only way to true freedom in your life.

Exercise 3

Take some time to think about the people who have hurt you. You may want to write a list of names. How do you begin to address such a tender and painful area of your life? Here are a few ideas to consider. Write a letter to the person. Your first draft should be written in a free style manner, meaning, do not worry about the spelling, punctuation marks, or whether you have run on sentences. Just get all those things you are feeling about the person written down. After you finish your first draft, do not look at it for a day.

On day two, look over the draft and revise it if necessary. Now read it out loud to an empty room. Getting those thoughts out of you and into the air will hopefully help you to feel better. The next step requires you to place the letter in a safe place until you are ready to forgive the person. You will have to determine if you want to share your letter with the person. Whatever decision you make, after you have forgiven the person, destroy or delete any extra copies of the letter and move on with your life. Life is too short to stay stuck in a bad place.

Another suggestion is to place two chairs in a room facing each other about three to five feet apart. Sit in one chair and imagine the person you need to forgive is sitting across from you in the second chair. Take a moment to breathe in and out so that you can collect your thoughts. Say whatever you need to say to that person; don't hold back. Expressing your anger, frustration, and hurt can help you to heal.

Use "I" statements, such as:

I felt hurt when you...

I was angry when you...

I was so disappointed by...

This is your time to express how you feel. After you complete this process, make sure to ask for a hug from someone who knows what you are going through and is supportive.

A third option is to request a time to meet with the person. This will take a great deal of courage. Dealing with conflict is not easy. What if the conversation turns into an argument? What if the person does not appear for your meeting? What if the person brings a third party to the meeting?

All these things must be taken into consideration. You will know if the person is ready to accept responsibility for the hurt they have caused you when they arrive on time, listen, sit upright, maintain an open posture and eye contact as well as respond to you in a respectful manner. Hopefully, at the end of the conversation the person will say they're sorry.

Forgiveness does not require that you tolerate unacceptable behavior from others. So, if you find yourself entering into a space of despair, heartache, or rage, please stop this process and seek some professional and/or spiritual help. There is no need to hurt yourself or anyone else. These exercises may require a great deal of time and energy to complete. Take your time and be gentle with yourself and others.

What if the person you want to forgive died before you had a chance to speak to them? I usually set aside at least twenty minutes to think about the person and at the end of the session, ask God to help me to forgive said person. I use the same process when I do not have the courage or desire to deal directly with the person if they are still alive. Life is a messy endeavor. Sometimes I know exactly where I am going. Other times, I am lost for a while. When you have done the best that you could do, that's good enough. Give yourself credit and move on.

Regardless of when the hurt occurred, ask God to help you to forgive each and every person who hurt you. It is not important that they ask for forgiveness. It is not essential that they know you have forgiven them. The divine habit of forgiveness is a beautiful gift that you give to yourself. Please do not forget to forgive yourself. No one is perfect. Life gets better when we extend ourselves enough grace to see ourselves as imperfect beings who are trying to become an improved version of yourself each day. As you forgive each person on your list, put a check mark by their name, then move on to the next person. You may need to skip over a few names because they will require a greater amount of time and attention. But be sure to finish your list. Hopefully, in time you will be able to put a check mark by each name. Now, it's time to roll up your sleeves and go to the next step on your journey.

Chapter 4

Think

"**F**or God has not given us a spirit of fear, but of power and of love and a sound mind."
II Timothy 1:7 (NKJV)

About thirty years ago, while working in a management level position at an educational institution, I created a one-word sign and placed it on my desk so that it was one of the first things a person saw when they came into my office. The word was *Think*.

Webster's dictionary defines think as to: exercise the power of reason; to weigh or consider. I found that human nature was such that people would not take the time to think about solutions to their problems, but instead rely on those who are known to be problem solvers.

It is important that we all develop problem solving skills. This skill is useful in all areas of our lives. I was hoping my sign would jump start some kind of subliminal message in their subconscious to have at least one or two solutions to discuss instead of just looking at me for the answers.

Several years after I placed the sign on my desk, a co-worker told me she had not understood why I had the sign on my desk. Later in life, she said she began to understand and thought about making her own "think" sign to put on her desk. I did not encourage or discourage her. I agreed it was good practice for people to see words and ponder their meaning. I also smiled because I do believe my sign had a positive impact on our office environment. I noticed that my other coworkers offered more solutions when discussing problems. It also helped when I asked them their thoughts concerning a particular project or issue.

Thinking can require a great deal of time and energy. Some of us speak before we think. Others do things without thinking. Most of the time these actions lead to disastrous results. I believe Reverend Martin Luther King Jr. said it best. "Rarely do we find men who willingly engage in hard, solid thinking. There is an almost universal quest for easy answers and half-baked solutions. Nothing pains some people more than having to think."

This is a sad, but true statement. Thinking requires the intentional act of contemplating one or more possible solutions to a problem or dilemma. There are some of us who ask others for advice when trying to determine the solution to a problem. Advice is okay, but it does not absolve you of the duty of thinking! Implementing someone else's solution can lead to some very unfortunate consequences if you have not taken the time to think it through.

Speaking of taking your time, two years ago my husband's, James's, car started having some major mechanical problems. He got several quotes from local auto mechanic shops to fix the problems. We were at the point where we needed to decide whether to repair the car at a cost of approximately $2,000 or buy another car. Fortunately, we had started saving money, given the age of our cars, and knowing that more repairs were in our future. After James and I thought over all of our options and what we could afford to do, we decided to buy another car.

We decided to look for a gently used SUV since we had a sedan. We did not care about the color or luxury amenities. We were looking for a basic SUV to get us around the city. We then looked at our savings accounts and budget to determine what we could afford to spend. After some discussion, we came up with an amount that we both could live with, and James spent several days reviewing the inventory for used vehicles on various websites.

Three different dealerships within 25 miles from our house had an SUV that met our needs, so after researching consumer related websites and automobile magazines, we scheduled an appointment to see and test drive each vehicle. We then contacted a local AAA affiliated auto mechanic shop near the respective dealership to schedule a AAA prepurchase inspection. The cost was less than $100.00 for most AAA members and their 86-point inspection was quite thorough. We also read the Google reviews for each of the dealerships.

I cannot overstate how valuable the Google reviews were to our family. After test driving each vehicle, the dealerships agreed to allow us to take the SUV to the local AAA auto mechanic shop for an inspection. As a side note, I do not recommend purchasing a vehicle from a dealership or person that will not allow you to take it for an independent inspection.

Two of the SUVs had so many repair issues that we could not wait to return them to the dealerships. The third vehicle appeared to be in good condition, so we obtained a CarFax report for it. After receiving the CarFax report via email and reviewing it, we decided to buy the third SUV. Just think, if we had bought one of the other two vehicles, it would have cost us a great deal of heartache and money.

Before you begin the process of thinking, you may have to

clean house, i.e. remove the negative thoughts in your mind and get rid of the naysayers. Instead, take a note from the apostle Paul. "And do not be conformed to this world, but be transformed by the renewing of your mind, that you may prove what is that good and acceptable and perfect will of God." Romans 12:2 (NKJV)

If you only know or feel comfortable with your negative thoughts then it's time to shift your paradigm, change lanes, or put on a new attitude. Again, I must share something else that apostle Paul said concerning how to change our negative thoughts into positive ones. "Finally, brethren, whatever things are true, whatever things are noble, whatever things are just, whatever things are pure, whatever things are lovely, whatever things are of good report, if there by any virtue, and if there be anything praiseworthy – meditate on these things." Philippians 4: 8 (NKJV)

For most of my life I was an anti-gun advocate. After too many killings of African Americans including Trayvon Martin, Tamir Rice, and Breonna Taylor, I realized that I did not feel safe in my own city or country. It was time for a change. I had to think about my options for providing better protection for me and my family. Four years ago, James and I signed up for a Carrying a Concealed Weapon (CCW) Class and applied to get our licenses to carry. We had to wait several months to get them, but it was worth it.

Although I was still very apprehensive about weapons, I wanted to be able to protect those I love, so James thought it was a good idea to go to visit a shooting range because the CCW Class offered less than an hour of practice at the shooting range. James knew I needed to be in a place where I felt safe and could receive further professional instructions.

My shooting is improving each month. It is most unfortunate what innocent and law-abiding citizens have to think about and do to protect their families and themselves, but this is our reality. I hope for a better tomorrow. Don't you?

How you perceive a situation makes a world of difference when deciding how you will handle that situation. If you have negative thoughts, they will surely lead to negative actions. Similarly, if you have positive thoughts, they will guide you to positive actions. A good life practice is to think before you say or do anything.

Exercise 4

Every now and then you should give yourself the gift of intentionally thinking about yourself. Let's practice this exercise today. Sit down at a desk or table. This is not the time to lay in bed and daydream. It is important to sit versus lay because we are about to get down to some serious business. Now, take some time to actually think about the problems or issues you are having in your life. Simply think about them for a while. By the way, you should not be doing anything else at this time, you should just be thinking.

After you have thought over your problems, and before you get weighed down in hopelessness, get a pen and paper, your tablet, cell phone, or whatever you use to take notes, and write down the problems that came to mind when you were thinking. Now, list some of the possible solutions to those problems. Be intentional about thinking about all the solutions. Even if the solutions sound bizarre, impossible, or simplistic, write them down. An ultimate solution may come from a compilation of several possible solutions. Your goal is to break through the barriers that are holding you back in life.

Remember, you are worth the time it takes to write down your thoughts, feelings, and needs. So, start writing. When you feel you have written down enough solutions, it will be time to move on to the next step of your journey.

Chapter 5

Plan

"For I know the plans I have for you, says the Lord. They are plans for good and not evil, to give you a future and a hope. In those days when you pray, I will listen. You will find me when you seek me, if you look for me in earnest."

Jeremiah 29:11-13 (TLB)

Now that you have thought about your problems, it is time to address them. I recommend keeping your list of solutions nearby so that you can review them as you move forward in your life. One of the most important questions you will have to ask yourself is, "What do I do first?"

Just as there are many ways to drive to your home, there may be several methods available to address your problems, but you must get started. I had a friend who often said, "If you fail to plan, then you plan to fail."

As you look over the possible solutions, determine which one addresses the most important problem in your life. This is the issue that should be addressed first. In our society, we do not like to deal with heavy and complicated problems, so we find ways to avoid them. But avoidance is never a good solution. The problems will remain, waiting for us to return. After you have determined which problem to address first, review your list of possible solutions. Do any of your solutions reasonably address the problem? In deciding whether or not a solution will make sense, I often go to God. Just as we discussed in the last chapter, when you think godly thoughts, they lead to godly plans. Do not be afraid to pray over your plans.

In II Chronicles, Chapter 20:12 (TLB), a war had been declared against the people of Judah by three other nations. Jehoshaphat, the king of Judah, was badly shaken and begged for help from God. He prayed, "O God, won't you stop them? We have no way to protect ourselves against this mighty army. We don't know what to do, but we are looking to you."

The chapter goes on to tell us that the Spirit of the Lord came upon one of the men standing there, Jahaziel. He told the people of Judah that the Lord said not to be afraid for the battle was not theirs, but God's. Jahaziel went on to tell them God's plans for dealing with the three other nations. He ended by reminding the people of Judah not to be afraid or discouraged, for God was with them.

If a king understood the need to pray and ask God for help, should we not also do the same thing when making our plans? A church member said that the word "Bible" was an acronym for:

Basic

Instructions

Before

Leaving

Earth

After Devlin moved out of our house, I recognized that I had never really lived on my own. After high school I went to college where I lived in a dorm. After college I had returned home and lived with my parents. I moved out of my parent's house when I got married to Devlin and we lived on the second floor of a two-family house. After Devlin moved out of our house, I was finally alone.

It would have been too easy to go back to my parents' house or sleep on a friend's sofa for a few weeks. I did not call anyone because I needed this time alone. I determined that I just needed to make it through the first night. After making it through my first night, my first work week, and my first month alone, I could exhale. I had to create a new life for myself. It took some time, and I made a lot of mistakes, but that's a part of life.

I had to stop running and prepare for the possible road ahead of me. During my second month of living on my own, I finally told my parents, a few relatives and some close friends about my separation from Devlin. I was surprised at the number of people who felt this was a good decision for both of us.

Some of the things I did during this time was to read numerous articles on separation and divorce. I also had conversations with family members and friends who had gone through a similar situation. I appreciated their candor. A few of them said they would pray for the reconciliation of our marriage. I cried many a tear during those first few months. Devlin and I had some good times. He was not only my husband, but he had been my friend.

I made a point of continuing to enjoy my life, which for me, included going to live music events, dining out at local independent restaurants, and watching comedy shows from the 70s and 80s.

As you formulate your plans, seek guidance from God and His Word. The Bible is as relevant today as it was 2,000 years ago. There is nothing new happening in this world that is a surprise to God. Additionally, seek out the support and advice from wise and mature Christians. "Where there is no counsel, the people fail; but in the multitude of counselors there is safety." Proverbs 11:14 (NKJV)

Do you have people in your life that you not only trust, but who offer you good, intelligent, reliable, and honest advice? If so, discuss your problems with them but under no circumstances should you discuss your problems with negative and immature people. They will only help you stay in the city called "pity" where there is no real life for you. Also stay away from those who tend to agree with whatever you say. One of you in this world is more than enough.

Be cautious when sharing your problems with neighbors, coworkers, or the cashier at your local grocery store, especially if those people are more acquaintances than friends or confidants. As interesting as the conversation might be, be careful not to accept or share personal and confidential information with others whom you consider to be acquaintances.

You must also take the time to listen to, and not just hear, what you think the Lord, your family and friends are telling you to do. There were times when I got so caught up in my own solution to a problem that although you may have thought I was listening to you, I was not! I was simply waiting for the right time to restate my solution. Then, there have been other times where I have inferred what I wished to believe from someone's comments. Have you ever done that? It can make your life and the lives of those around you very chaotic and dysfunctional. When you listen, listen with an intent to understand what the other person is saying to you. A good habit to develop is to repeat back to the person what you believe they are saying to you. This is an essential element of good communication. They may have some great advice to offer you, but if you choose not to listen, you will miss out.

If your plans make sense to you, then the next question you

need to ask yourself is, "Do I have what I need to implement this plan?"

Sometimes I come up with a great plan, but I do not have the skills, money, time, or energy to implement it. It is important to have a realistic plan that works for you. If you do not have the resources you need to address your problem, you will not be successful. Benjamin Franklin said, "By failing to prepare, you are preparing to fail."

I started dating James about ten years after my divorce from Devlin. James and I were engaged for two years. After the second year, my family and friends started asking if we had selected a date. It wasn't James who was reluctant to set a date; it was me. I was the indecisive one in the relationship. After going through one bad marriage, I was a bit skittish about jumping the broom a second time.

We decided to marry in July 2020. Each month in the fall of 2019 we were asked if we had a specific date selected so that people could check their schedules. We did not have a date. By December 2019 I knew I was in trouble because I had not shopped for my wedding dress, compiled a guest list, contacted the church to see if it was available, or booked the reception venue. I had barely thought about a color scheme, florist, photographer, or DJ. I now see why people hire wedding coordinators. They are essential to a flawless wedding day.

My mother called up a special person to help me. Help came in the form of an extraordinary wedding coordinator, my niece, Hope. What I could not get accomplished in the previous six months, Hope put together in six weeks. From the beginning of January to mid-February, we reserved the church, reception venue, and DJ. The wedding invitations were ordered and the list of photographers were ready to be contacted by the end of the month. And, after trying on over ten wedding dresses, I found the one! My measurements were taken and the dress was scheduled to arrive for my final fitting in April.

I felt like a great burden had been lifted from my shoulders. There were still a few minor things to take care of, but for the most part, we were in good place. Then, March of 2020 came and with it, a virus called COVID-19 turned the world upside down. The virus allegedly started in China and quickly spread throughout the world. By the third week of March, the United States was shut down due to the millions of people who were either sick or dying from the virus. The hospitals and staff were overworked and underpaid. Everyone was sent home and told to stay in their houses. The workforce had to adapt to working from home and learning how to use Zoom daily. It was so eerie to see streets quiet at 2:00 pm, cars parked in their driveways all day, mall parking lots empty, and no one walking around their neighborhoods. Parents had to figure out how to watch their children who were home all day and work at the same time. Visits to family members were not encouraged, given the fact that we had no idea how to contain this virus. Some entities, such as churches, refused to close their doors and remained open throughout the COVID-19 pandemic.

I did not know what to do. We had planned on inviting approximately 125 guests. I suggested to James that we post-pone the wedding until 2021 because I did not want anyone getting sick or dying because they had attended our wedding. He thought we should stick with our original plans. My thoughts and prayers were all over the place. Finally, James agreed to postpone the wedding. Our hope was that by 2021, there would be a cure for COVID-19 and therefore, it would be safe for everyone to be together again.

When I told my mother about the postponement of our wedding, she listened quietly. Then she asked, "What if next year is the same as this year?"

I did not have an answer to her question. I was so confused. I knew that other people had planned their weddings in 2020, so I read several articles to see what course of action they were taking to protect their guests and have a lovely day. As I grappled with what to do, James reminded me that our wedding was about two people who loved each other, pledging their lives to one another before God and others. We did not need to have a long dress, 125 guests, and a chicken dinner to have a wedding. His words and my mother's unanswered question brought clarity to me in a very uncertain time in the world.

We reviewed our wedding plans and decided to proceed with our special day. However, we reduced the number of guests to thirty-five, had everyone wear a mask, and held the ceremony and reception at the church. James and I had a small and beautiful wedding. Although our wedding day was different than originally planned, the love, support, and joy were present throughout the day. We were very grateful that no one caught the COVID-19 virus as a result of attending our wedding.

Get prepared! You are worth it. You may have to dig down deep within yourself to develop the skills and talents you need to address the problem. You may also have to ask for some help. My mother was in charge of a family event 40 years ago. She was attempting to make sure everything was in order at a banquet hall. She was getting tired and frustrated, but there were still so many little things left to do. A friend of our family, Mr. Clark, had been observing my mother for a few minutes. Mr. Clark went over to ask if she was okay. He further stated that my mother looked a little frustrated.

Mom went over the list of things that remained to be completed before the event was scheduled to start. Mr. Clark looked at Mom and told her that all she had to do was ask for some help. There were people all around her who were ready, able, and willing to help her. She forgot the simple act of asking for help. By doing so, it lightened her burden so she could enjoy the event.

Finally, don't be bashful about seeking guidance from God. After all, He is the Master Planner. No plan is perfect, so be prepared to make the necessary adjustments day by day. One Saturday morning I was thinking over the things I wanted to get done that day. I wrote down several errands on my to do list and imagined the route I would take to get to each location. Then, I thought about the amount of time I would spend at each stop. After I had gotten dressed, God asked me to rearrange my schedule. I thought to myself, "What? This schedule will work because it makes sense. It puts everything in a logical order."

He then told me that I needed to do the most important thing first.

I surrendered that day and my schedule to God; it was one of the best decisions I had ever made. It was a productive day. It was also a day where I remembered being present in the moment and not just rushing through my to do list. It helped me to appreciate being able to engage with other people, drive around, shop, and enjoy the sunshine.

As I reflected on my day later that night, I realized that God was asking me to put first things first. Sometimes I do put the most important things first, but most of the time I put fun things first. Then, there are other times where I put selfish things first.

As you plan, think about how you can use your resources, such as time, money, and energy, in the most efficient and effective ways. Keep yourself open and your plans flexible so that there will be room to shift, grow, and make changes as needed.

Exercise 5

Write! Yes, here we go again with that action verb. First, determine what is the problem. What do you need to fix? How are you going to complete the project? Then, start to write your action plan to help you get to the finish line. Think of your plan the way you would give someone directions to your house. The starting point would be where they live, and the end point would be your house. You would have to provide enough details so that the person would not get lost or go to the wrong address. Just as there are several different ways to go from place A to place B, make sure your plan is flexible enough so that when you need to shift gears or slow down, you will not stop. Is this step necessary? Yes. Will it take some time? Yes. Does it hurt sometimes? Yes. Will you be glad you did it? Yes.

No plan is perfect. The important thing is to start somewhere and get moving. By the way, if you do not think that your plan has a possibility of being successful, then do not expect anyone else to join you. If you do not believe in yourself, why should anyone else? Believe in yourself. Believe in your plan.

Believe that what appears to be impossible today, just might be possible tomorrow. Believe that better days are ahead for you.

Whatever you do, do not give up. One of my good friends ends her letters, notes, and emails with a quote from Robert Browning. "The best is yet to be."

I do believe the best is yet to be.

Chapter 6

Do

"Moses spoke to the people: "Don't be afraid. Stand firm and watch God do his work of salvation for you today. Take a good look at the Egyptians today for you're never going to see them again. God will fight the battle for you. And you? You keep your mouths shut! God said to Moses: "Why cry out to me? Speak to the Israelites. Order them to get moving." Exodus 14:13-15 (MSG)

When preparing to do a difficult task, I have found it helpful to do the hardest part first. Why? Because human nature is such that if we do the easy things first, we may tend to hesitate or stop when it comes to the difficult parts of a project. When you get the hard parts out of the way first, it makes it easier to continue with the easy parts.

I once read an article about getting fit and looking good. One of the suggestions was to cut out a photograph of someone else's body from a magazine that I thought looked great and then tape a photograph of your face on top of that body. I did this and taped the altered photograph on the inside of my kitchen pantry door.

That photograph stayed on my kitchen pantry door for more than a year and I did not come close to reshaping my body to match the image in that photograph. Why? I did not make a habit of following the other suggestions in the article, such as exercising and eating foods that were delicious, nutritious, and good for my body. I could have looked at that photograph every day for the next five years and my body would have stayed the same. In order to have a more fit and shapely body, I needed to implement all the changes suggested in the article. I also needed to change my mindset from, "I can't do it" to, "Yes, I can and yes, I will do it starting today."

After you have determined what you need to do first, get moving! Every day you wait to start your plan is a day that you have wasted and will never get back. The first few steps may be very difficult, but that is why it is so important to surround yourself with positive supporters.

In the 1980s my brother, John, went missing for several weeks. One day he just left home and did not return. After twenty-four hours, my mother contacted the police department. When the police arrived at our home, they made my parents feel like they were criminals. They asked such questions as, "Why did John leave? What happened here? Did John do this often?"

My mother was greatly concerned because my brother took several medications which he needed each day. In spite of the police officer's behavior, my mother made them complete a missing person's report. My mother then called our local, county, and state public officials to seek their assistance. She did not get much of a response from any of them but that did not stop her from asking for their help as she prayed for John's safe return home.

John was located several weeks later in a town about thirty minutes from our home. He had wandered away from home and somehow ended up in a nearby city. After the police found him walking around in their town John was placed in the county jail. The police department in the next county contacted my mother. She had to once again, call and write to several politicians for help to get John out of jail. Through God's divine love and intervention, several other people who had heard about our plea to get John home stepped in to help our family. Most of them were strangers who simply wanted to help a hurting family. John returned home a few weeks later. We were all so happy to see him. John being found and returned home was possible because of a mother's love and determination to do something.

I was traveling one summer and I thought I was following the GPS directions. However, I missed a turn. I knew I was going in the wrong direction because the lady's voice on the GPS kept repeating the words, "Wrong turn. Recalibrating directions."

What that GPS was telling me was that, although I had made a wrong turn, it was going to get me back on track so I could still arrive at the correct destination. Just like when we make a wrong turn in a car, we may make mistakes when implementing our plans. If a part of your plan does not work, get rid of it. Revise the plan so that you can keep moving forward. No plan is perfect. All plans usually require revisions. Please don't let perfectionism keep you from the finish line.

As you complete each phase of your plan, you will gain more confidence in pressing on. If you encounter a large pothole, you may be able to go around it or gently roll over it, however, if you see it at the last second, you will hit it and this could cause some major damage to your car. Are your plans like a car, stopped forever? No way.

Sometimes we must do what seems impossible but is necessary. This is how I felt as my family took care of my father the last eighteen months of his life.

My father could be defined as a man's man. He was strong, steely eyed and had a no-nonsense personality. Dad worked hard and played hard. He demanded respect from his family members and close friends. He mowed his lawn in the summer and cleared the snow from the driveway in the winter with his snowplow. My father was fortunate to have led a very active life for eighty years.

Dad was employed in the construction industry for thirty years and after going over the same disputes with his supervisors concerning the treatment of minority employees, he decided to retire.

He continued to help with repair projects on most of our family member's houses, including installing toilets and hot water tanks, repairing steam heating systems, and placing glass block windows in the basement.

One of his major projects involved demolishing his one car garage and building a brick two car garage. Dad would walk around the house several times a year to check for any problems. My parents owned several rental properties and their tenants never wanted to move because my parents took good care of them by repairing problems quickly and efficiently.

Dad's favorite hobbies included hunting, fishing, and traveling. While in good health, he and my mother traveled to Hawaii, Aruba, and Mexico in addition to taking several cruises with friends.

2016 brought about several health challenges for my family. While on a summer trip, we noticed that the right side of Dad's face near his jaw line was swollen. We asked him if he was in any pain and he said no.

I thought there might be something wrong with his dentures

or gums so my mother said that they would make a doctor's appointment when we returned to Ohio.

At the end of August, my father went to see a doctor, where they performed a biopsy of his nasal cavity. The diagnosis was that Dad had squamous cell carcinoma, a type of cancer in his sinus area. The oncologist recommended surgery and radiation so Dad's surgery was scheduled for the second week in October. Afterwards, his body was allowed to heal for six weeks.

From December 2016 to mid-January of 2017, my parents were at the hospital 5 days a week for his radiation treatments, which caused a large black blotch to appear on his face; he detested that patch. After the radiation treatments were finished, Dad decided not to have any additional treatments for his cancer. He felt that if the surgery and radiation had not cured him, then he would live with whatever was happening in his body.

The doctors made several attempts to change his mind but after the third or fourth conversation on this matter, my family intervened and told the medical staff, "No means no."

Dad did not want to be a test subject; he wanted to live out his last days in his way so when my father refused further invasive treatments it seemed like the doctors gave up on him and us. There was never any discussion about holistic options, which may have had a gentler effect on his body.

As the spring and fall of 2017 came and went, I saw the changes in my father. Dad was losing his appetite and as a result, he was shrinking before my eyes. He walked slower and slept longer. He was unable to complete routine home repairs, go hunting, or fishing. What really hurt him was the realization that he could no longer mow his lawn.

I had been contemplating retirement from my current job for several years. Each year I delayed it for financial or medical reasons. As I saw my father's health deteriorating, I decided in the it was time to say goodbye to the workforce. I retired at the end of the year in 2017 to spend time with my father and help my mother. It is a decision I have never regretted.

Dad made it through January 2018, but each day presented a new set of challenges for him. He wasn't used to sitting around and became very frustrated at times. After all, he was used to being able to do everything without help. Not being able to drive his pick-up truck or use his snowplow was hard for him. We had to bring in other family members and friends to complete repairs around the house.

My father's birthday was in June and for the past 10 years we had hosted a large family gathering which included a cook-out, fish fry, music, and dancing to celebrate his birthday. In February, my mother recommended I contact my brothers, Lenny and Miles, who resided outside of Ohio to suggest they not wait until June for their family visit this year.

Lenny and Miles arrived in Ohio three weeks later. We had our family celebration indoors but it was wonderful weekend. They got to spend some one-on-one time with Dad. It was the last time they saw Dad alive.

During the last four weeks of my father's life, he required around the clock care. His insurance provided compassionate and respectful hospice care services but my mother did not like too strangers in her house or too many people touching her man. Since she had a close relationship with most of her children, grandchildren, and great grandchildren, she asked her great-grand son, Quincy, if he was interested in helping her take care of Dad. He said he was not sure what to do but he would try to help. Mom and Quincy were an amazing care team who made sure Dad was clean, comfortable, and received his medications on time. I often marveled at Quincy's reliability. He was a recent high school graduate who could have chosen to do other things but each day he showed up and was prepared to do anything that Mom requested of him.

When we were confused by all the medical jargon, we looked to Hope, for interpretation and instructions since she was a nurse. She often stopped by to check on Dad and us and gave us such comfort with just her presence.

Mom and Dad also enjoyed their granddaughter, Faith's, visits. Her witty personality and smile lit up the room.

I and other family members were a part of the relief team who took over so that Mom and Quincy could get some rest, do their errands, or simply take a few minutes to look out the window.

I have been journaling for most of my life, not on a routine basis, but I have enough notes to fill up several three ring binders and folders. I recently looked through one of my binders and found several entries written around the time of Dad's last days and shortly after his death. Here are a few excerpts.

* * *

Morning Light
   March 2018
   As I watched my brother escort my Dad to bed, my Dad said something to the effect of, "It won't be like this for long..."

   And I thought, "Dad you are right, it may not always be this way."

   When I woke up the next morning at my parent's house, I looked into my father's room. I saw the top half of Dad's body on the bed and the lower half dangling near the floor.

   I said, "Good morning," and asked what he was trying to do.

   Dad said he was trying to sit up to see what time it was from his clock on the dresser. I told him it was 7 am. Dad said it was still early. I asked if I could help him back to bed and he said yes.

I gently moved the top portion of his body up towards the pillows and shifted his legs back onto the bed and covered him up. As I looked at Dad, that's when I knew...more changes were coming. But God is already there.

Unconditional and Amazing

March 2018

When I think about my mother I think about love, laughter, joy, and hope. I think about anchors, life jackets and safety nets, for that is what she has been for our family. What is most wonderful is her love. Her love for God. Her love for her children, grandchildren, great grandchildren, other relatives, and friends. And her love for her husband of sixty-four years. It is an unconditional and amazing love. To have experienced it for sixty plus years is nothing short of marvelous. Here's to unconditional and amazing love. If you have not found it, may it find you.

Open Door Policy

March 2018

When I was young, all I wanted to do was to have my privacy. I lived in a small house with a large family that included two parents and seven children. There was not much space for privacy, except in the bathroom! And you could not stay in the bathroom long because someone else always needed to use it.

With my Dad being ill, I stay at my parent's house overnight several times a month. There are so many things going on with doctor's appointments, repairs, and visitors coming in every week. My Dad goes to bed each night around 7 pm but has been known to get up early. We recently had to stop him from trying to get up and go into the basement for some reason. He finally stopped when we closed the door to the basement stairway.

At night I try to stay up to make sure Dad is okay. It is a new way of living; it is a new way of thinking. It is a new way of caring about a parent. When I am with my parents I feel like I need to protect them from the outside world and at other times, from themselves. They are smaller, weaker, and more vulnerable. I don't want anything to happen to them. I don't want anyone to hurt them.

So lately, I have been sleeping with my door open. Now I have an open-door policy so that I can hear my Dad sleep, get up, move around, cough, snore, sigh, and rest. If he rests too much I am afraid he is dead because he is so still. Some days he tries to stay up to spend time with us but it is a losing battle.

Here's to my new open-door policy.

The Slow Race
March 2018

Thump...shuffle...thump...shuffle...thump...shuffle. That is the new rhythm of my Dad's walk. He started using a cane for the first time in his life in March 2018. He held off using one for as long as he could. But finally, due to the unbalanced nature of his gait, he had to use the cane in order to safely get around the house. It was strange at first, watching him use his cane. Truth be told, it is still strange.

Thump...shuffle...thump...shuffle...thump...shuffle. My Dad cannot pick up his feet very high. He lets his feet glide across the floor, about a half inch above ground. The cane adds its own harmony to his new walk. I am so accustomed to seeing my Dad as this vibrant active talkative man who was my hero. Now he seems resigned...to his body betraying him by slowing down...to Mom taking care of his daily meals...to death. Personally, I think he has invited death to come and visit him soon. My Dad always said he never wanted to be sick with all these tubes in his body and unaware of what is going on around him. We are trying to honor his wishes. But through no fault of his or ours, he is slowly and ever so gently slipping away.

Aging is a bittersweet process. Everyone does not get to make it to their fifties, sixties, seventies, eighties, or nineties. But for those who do, they encounter a unique set of difficulties. As I watch my parents age, I see their mortality more and more and I also see mine. I selfishly want to keep them here forever or at least one day longer than my life. So, as I listen to my Dad's new rhythm, thump...shuffle...thump...shuffle, I wait. I wait to see if he has made it to his destination safely, be it the bathroom, kitchen, bedroom or garage. I wait to see if he is unbalanced, trips, or worse case, falls. I wait to see if he will safely return to his special spot on the sofa where he can watch a western show or movie.

This is the new rhythm in our lives. How long I hear it, I don't know. Maybe Dad will move on to using a walker or a wheelchair. The silence of not hearing Dad move around in this world in some way, shape, or form is something I do not want to think about right now. For now, I take comfort in hearing his thump...shuffle...thump...shuffle...thump...shuffle.

Are You Ready

April 2018

I was looking at one of my text messages. The first line of the message read, "Are you ready?"

I usually think about this question in reference to salvation. However, this week when I read the text, it had another meaning. As I watch my father's health decline each day, our time together becomes even more precious. I almost don't want to leave him for a day because I know when I return, he will have further declined into a smaller and weaker man. So, I read this text from a different perspective. It is not about if Dad is ready to leave us. He has been sick for over a year. He knows his body. He knows what is working and not working. He knows how he hopes his journey in this life will end. Dad has a plan.

That statement was for me and maybe some of my family members. Are we ready to let go of Dad? Am I ready to tell him it is okay to rest? Am I ready to say an earthly goodbye? Am I ready to cry at the loss of the most consistent male figure in my life? Am I ready to give Dad back to the One who loaned him to us for eighty plus years? Am I ready? I don't think I am today. Maybe, just maybe, tomorrow.

Last Breath

May 2018

It has been several weeks since I felt like writing. My Dad died on April 14, 2018. Can we ever prepare ourselves for the death of a loved one? Probably not. Even as I saw my Dad dying, I was not ready for his death. But death comes a calling anyway. The last days of my father's life were sad. He stopped eating two weeks before his death. Dad stopped talking to us one week before his death. He stopped drinking fluids three days before his death. The last few days of his life he slept like a baby. During the last three days of Dad's life, his breathing slowed down and could barely be heard.

April 8 was an exhausting week for my family. By April 11, I suggested to my mother that we have Dad taken to a nursing home for respite care. She agreed and we made arrangements for Dad to picked up on April 13. Dad left home on a sunny Friday morning. I remember my mother saying that Dad would never make it back home. The ambulance staff gently lifted Dad's frail little body on a sheet and placed him in the ambulance. I kissed Dad on his forehead and told him we would see him soon. When we got to the nursing home Dad was in fresh pajamas and resting in his hospital bed.

One of the nurses told us that Dad would probably not make it through the weekend and that we should notify Dad's other family members and friends to visit him soon. Dad had already signed a do-not-resuscitate (DNR) order years ago. We knew what he wanted and planned on following his orders.

There were so many visitors that the nursing home staff had to bring in additional chairs. As more visitors arrived, we ran out of space in Dad's room so they had to wait outside in the lounge until someone left. We all gathered around him for the next 36 hours. We laughed. We talked. We sang. We hugged.

Most of our family members and friends had left by 9 pm on Saturday night. There were four of us left: Mom, me, and my two nieces, Faith and Hope.

I asked Mom if she was ready to leave. She said no. She had been sitting by my Dad's right side all day on Friday and Saturday. I noticed Dad's breathing was becoming shallower. I asked Faith to play some blues music for Dad on her cell phone. She found some music and we watched Dad as the music played. Shortly after 10 pm, Hope checked Dad's feet. She told us that Dad would probably not need any more medication.

We talked softly and watched Dad. His breathing was so soft and gentle. A little after 10 pm, Dad let out one final soft and gentle breath and then he was gone. Dad's mouth had been slightly opened the last few days. Mom pressed his lips together. He was smiling at us. At least that is what I choose to believe. I thought Dad's last hours would be terrible, harsh, painful, and scary. They were not. It was peaceful. He had four women who loved him by his side. He did not die at home. I think that was a gift from God to Mom. I thank God that I had the privilege of being by my father's side when he left earth to go back home to heaven.

God knew what we needed and gave it to us, to let Dad go in a peaceful manner. We had done our best. Dad got to live and die on his own terms. I have no regrets. I have plenty of good memories and I know where my father is. My Dad's last breath was the beginning of a new kind of normal for all of us who loved him. That last breath covered eighty-two years of life, sixty-four years of marriage and raising seven children, and numerous grandchildren and great grandchildren. That last breath was a sweet goodbye. Thank you, Lord, for peaceful last breaths. They are gifts from heaven.

* * *

My mother and our family are continuing our healing journey. We try to take life one day at a time. We remember the good times we had with Dad. When I look around our homes I see Dad's work in a kitchen project, basement repair, or the two-car garage. Several of our family members have his personality. We are grateful that Dad was allowed to die with dignity and in peace. God has a way of easing our pain each day. Dad now gets to watch over us in heaven.

When you do what you need to do and don't run from the pain and sorrow, you will find a strength you never knew you had. Our story reminds me of a scripture I read in the book of I Kings. Chapter 18 talks about the prophet Elijah, who was given a special strength in the Lord.

"And soon the sky was black with clouds. A heavy wind brought a terrific rainstorm and Ahab left quickly for Jezreel. Then the Lord gave special strength to Elijah. He tucked his cloak into his belt and ran ahead of Ahab's chariot all the way to the entrance of Jezreel." I Kings 18:45-46 (NLT)

There will be times on your journey when you will need a special kind of strength to accomplish the things you are trying to do. Please ask other people for help. We, as humans, were not designed to handle life and all of its problems on our own. Ask God for help. He is able and willing to help us each day of our lives.

I am truly encouraged by my mother, Quincy, Faith, and Hope. There are so many people doing such courageous things to keep pressing on. Their courage gives people like me the tenacity to get up and move on to the next phase in my plan.

Exercise 6

After you have written down your plan or plans, look them over to determine your first step. What do you need to do first? There is no magic here. Review your plans until you are comfortable with a defined set of actions. Personally, I like to organize my plans in steps or phases. For example, when I am preparing my tax return, the first step for me is to look at my previous year's tax return. As the new year begins, my second step is to find an envelope to place all the tax documents I will be receiving in the mail for the next two to six weeks. The third step involves looking through my financial, medical, and other records to see if there are any additional documents to include in this year's tax return. The fourth step is to put all the documents in some kind of order for my final review.

Like preparing a tax return, your plan will take some time and energy. I recommend that you set aside at least one hour per day to work on your plan. You may want to write your first step on Post-it Notes and place them in several places around your home so that you can see them every day, such as your bathroom mirror, refrigerator door, or night stand. This will hopefully inspire you to stay focused. Another idea is to block out some time on your cell phone or wall calendar. If you do not make time to complete each step, your plan will surely fail.

Your plan may require the assistance of other people and resources. How are you at networking? Do you maintain healthy and helpful relationships? Is there someone in your life who can be a mentor? How is your health and your finances? Have you done any research on the areas of your plan where you lack knowledge? Are you willing to ask a close and trustworthy relative or friend to be your accountability partner? This would be the person who has the right to ask you how your plan is coming along, and you must be honest with your response.

Can you honestly say that you are willing do what it takes to make your plan a success? Make sure you check to make sure you have the resources you need for each step in your plan.

When you have completed step one, take a break and determine what is needed for step two. Don't be hurried. Be thoughtful in how you use your time, resources, and energy. Imagine how you will feel when you have worked through your problem. Let that positive energy keep replenishing you so that you will be eager to start the next step in your plan.

Your plan may take a week, month, or a year to complete. But guess what. If you don't get started, you will never finish. When you are fearful, tired, or discouraged, find someone or something to give you the support you need to press on. If you fall down, get back up. Don't wallow in your mistakes, for this will take time away from you meeting your goals. However, if you find yourself making too many costly mistakes or getting overwhelmed, take a break. Sometimes taking a step away from the situation can give you a new perspective which will lead to some fresh and creative solutions.

Remember that there is no perfect plan, so you must be prepared to reassess your plan weekly, if not daily. There will be times when unforeseen events occur in your life, such as the death of a loved one, job loss, or illness. Do not be discouraged. Be present in those moments. Then, when the time is right, get back on track with your plan. Whatever you do – don't give up. If you keep on moving, before you know it, you will be at the finish line and stepping into the winner's circle.

Chapter 7

Celebrate

"Rather, you must seek the Lord your God at a place of worship He Himself will choose from among all the tribes-the place where His name will be honored....There you and your families will feast in the presence of the Lord your God and you will rejoice in all you have accomplished because the Lord your God, has blessed you.... You must celebrate there in the presence of the Lord your God with your sons and daughters and all your servants.

Deuteronomy 12:5, 7, 12A (NLT)

After you have diligently worked your plan and seen the results, it's time to celebrate. Celebrations can occur in so many different ways. I celebrate by doing things I enjoy, such as dancing, eating a good burger, or relaxing at a luxurious hotel, resort, or spa for a week or weekend. If you are unsure as to how you can celebrate, try doing simple things like walking in a local park or taking a bicycle ride around your neighborhood. You'll see things on foot or a bicycle that you miss when driving a car. Perhaps, eating a scoop of your favorite ice cream or watching the sunset is more your style. Whatever your preference, please just do something. If you don't know what you like to do to celebrate, now is a good time to put together a list of activities. Your future is bright. You will accomplish great things. Doesn't it make sense to have a list available of fun and happy things to do?

Remember in the beginning of Chapter 6 – DO, where I mentioned the photograph on my pantry door? Well, I eventually did something about my weight. I joined a group of women who were interested in developing healthier lifestyle habits. Our facilitator, June, was a humorous, knowledgeable, and organized young woman who met with us once a week for several years. At the beginning of each meeting, June would remind us that she had no medical background. She was just like us, someone searching for ways to enjoy a healthier lifestyle.

Every week, we weighed in before we began our session. June placed a scale a short distance away from the group so that she could see and discreetly write down our weight for that week. We discussed what things were working in our lives to become healthier individuals, as well as the things that hindered our progress. Whenever a new member joined the group, June asked them to keep a food journal. We also kept food journals. When I started writing down everything I ate in a week, I was surprised at the amount of food that went into my body.

June gave us articles, books, and tips on how to create an individualized meal plan that worked for our body type and lifestyle. My eating plan included more fresh fruit, vegetables, water, and limited amounts of red meats and fried foods. She also encouraged us to exercise based on our physical condition. I tried to walk at least thirty minutes each day and use my weights twice week. I saw results within three months. I felt lighter. I had more energy. My thoughts were clearer, and life was good.

After nine months of eating healthier foods, exercising, and thinking positive thoughts, it was time to celebrate. Since I did not want to waste calories, my favorite go to beverages became a glass of water or a cup of green tea. They were refreshing, invigorating, and good for my body.

Other times, I listened to several of my favorite songs as I danced around the house. I reached a place in my life where I enjoyed shopping again. I was bolder in my color choices and styles. I knew I was in a good place with my body when I could look at a pair of jeans, dress, or top on the hanger and know they would fit without trying them on. Oh happy day!

Speaking of happy, if you need a little help to get started with a celebration activity, listen and dance to the song *Happy* by Pharrell Williams. Don't just sit down and listen to it but actually get up and dance to the song. Once you get started, you will probably wonder why you did not think of that activity for yourself. But be careful because once you start dancing, you may not stop!

My sister-in-law, Cici, has themed celebration events each year. One year we celebrated the 1970s disco era. The guests wore big afro wigs, bell bottom pants, and shimmering tops. There is something about dancing to *Disco Inferno* in stack shoes that makes a child of the 70s smile.

Another year the theme was western attire. I put on my cowgirl hat and tied my bandana around my neck so I could giddy up and not be late for my date. The Great Gatsby theme was one of my favorites. Men wore suits with fedora hats. Ladies had on lots of pearls, gloves up to their elbows, and flapper dresses.

The next time you are invited to a themed celebration event, put together your outfit and go and have a ball. Cici's parties were always a big hit where the guests had a good time.

Dressing up is not just for children or Halloween, it is for anyone who dares to live it up and have some fun.

Another happy moment came for me through scripture. Zephaniah 3:17 (TLB) says: "For the Lord your God has arrived to live among you. He is a mighty Savior. He will give you victory. He will rejoice over you in great gladness; he will love you and not accuse you. Is that a joyous choir I hear? No, it is the Lord himself exulting over you in a happy song;"

Can you imagine God singing to you? I am certain that the words would be beautiful, and the melody would bring great joy to your soul.

Sometimes, when we get through some of the trials and challenges of life, we have to let other people know about what we have been through. This too, can be a form of celebration.

In the church world, we call this celebratory activity *testifying*. We all need to hear good news each day. Don't be ashamed to share your good news with other people. Don't be afraid to smile one of those big and beautiful ones that covers half of your face. Don't quench that joy which is bubbling up in your soul. Let it out. Let it go. Let it flow. Let it be.

I had an experience once where someone showed me a new way to celebrate life. I attended a church near my house and went to the 8 am service. In case I need to get up or leave early, I usually like to sit at the end of the pew. Well, the sanctuary began to fill up as more and more people came into the service. I was able to let one person go past me to a space in the center of my pew, but I was not so fortunate with the next person. When the usher asked if I could move over so that someone could sit on the end, I wanted to recite a speech that I had rehearsed just for the occasion. The high point of my speech involved me telling them that I was not going to move over. I would get up and let the person go past me to sit in the middle of the pew because I was determined to remain anchored in my end seat! Before I could begin my speech, the usher walked back to the vestibule to escort the person to my pew. So, I decided that I would just wait and tell both of them my thoughts on asking me to move over. I was getting all worked up and doing this self-righteous thinking during a church service. What can I say? I am a work in progress.

When the person came up to the pew, I instantly changed my mind about making a fuss about sitting on the end of the pew. I simply moved over towards the center of the pew as graciously as I could. After glancing at the man who would be sitting next to me, I realized he was a very special person. He was between 35 to 50 years of age and dressed in a nice suit. As he came towards the pew, I could see that he was paralyzed on the right side of his body. He walked with a limp and could only use his left side. However, he had the most amazing smile I had seen in a long time.

I never asked for his name, so I'll refer to him as Leo. He told me a part of his life's journey as we sat in the church service. Leo said he'd been shot in the head and run over by a car on the same day, several years ago. No one expected him to live, but here he was, sitting in a pew and praising God. When the choir sang, Leo moved his body from side to side, letting that choir know how much he appreciated their efforts. When the music director told the congregation to clap their hands, Leo proceeded to clap his left hand against his left thigh. If you ever wondered how a one-armed man claps, now you know!

Leo had a great laugh. At one point during the service the pastor said something so funny that Leo and I laughed as we leaned against each other. It was a beautiful service. I had the opportunity to worship with someone who truly knew what it meant to be a miracle in God's kingdom. I was blessed during this service because of God.

There is a saying that there will be people in your life for a reason or a season. I believe I met Leo for a reason. God knew it wasn't important where I sat in the church service. What *was* important was the condition of my heart and spirit. When I decided to be faithful to God in that service, he blessed my life as only He could.

I also had the blessed opportunity to meet a young lady named Bonnie. She and I had received scholarships to attend a high school in New York and we stayed in touch afterwards.

Bonnie is kind, intelligent, and a craftsperson extraordinaire. Throughout these past 45 years, we have been through births, moves, relationships, graduations, illnesses, and deaths. It is wonderful to have someone by your side, not just for the good times, but especially during the turbulent times in your life.

Several years ago, Bonnie wanted a better life for her family, so they packed up and moved to another state. What a journey- a major move with a new job and house, all while raising her teenage daughter. And now, Bonnie has met her Boaz—a man who loves God and her. That man, Daniel, asked Bonnie to marry him on one Mother's Day. That was such a memorable way to celebrate a special day.

One of the most unfortunate things I ever heard was from a person who did not celebrate his birthday. He further mentioned that no one celebrated his birthday for several years.

Don't wait for someone to do something to celebrate your life or success; do it for yourself. It is never too late to celebrate a birthday. I had the pleasure of attending several birthday celebrations in the past 16 months for three nonagenarians. In case you don't know, a nonagenarian is a person between the ages of 90 to 99.

The first celebration was for Sister Amie. Sister Amie and my mother met at church over twenty years ago. After my mother left that church, they remained friends and stayed in contact with each over throughout their friendship. Sister Amie was a delightful lady who kept up with the latest fashion trends and technology. Her family said that Sister Amie stayed up to date on current events through her Facebook account.

Sister Amie's family threw her a wonderful party at a local banquet hall decorated in navy blue and silver. The invitations were beautiful.

When Sister Amie entered the hall, over two hundred family members and friends stood up and clapped for her. She was escorted to her white and gold Queen Anne Throne chair in the center of the head table by her children. Even though we were only friends of Sister Amie, her family members made us feel welcomed and were so kind. The music was good, and the meal was enjoyable. Sister Amie gave a brief speech thanking everyone. I think she was looking forward to going home that evening so she could check her Facebook page to see what was being said about her celebration.

The second celebration was for Brother Louis. I met Brother Louis and his wife, Sister Louis, at church. The Louis' children held the ninetieth party at the Louis' home. The fifty plus guests were spread throughout the house. The black and gold decorations included birthday banners, plaques that stated what was going on the year Brother Louis was born, table favors, and large balloons. A local caterer provided a delicious meal.

Brother Louis received some great gifts- one of which was a roll of ninety lottery scratch off tickets. Brother Louis also said a brief and heartfelt speech. Although it has already been a year, I still find myself looking back at the photos I took at the party and smiling.

The third celebration was for someone close to my heart, my mother. She started off many of her conversations to me with the following words: I don't want a big celebration! As I thought about the other two nonagenarian celebrations, I wanted to do something on the same scale, if not bigger, but Mom said no. All she wanted to do was to go to her favorite restaurant and be surrounded by her children, grandchildren, and great grandchildren. That was enough for her so we honored her request.

Hope and I put up red and black decorations at her house the day before the dinner. She enjoyed the decorations, especially the three-foot-tall numbers. Gifts and calls were coming in all day long and later we took Mom to the casino for a few hours to start her birthday weekend off with a bang.

The day of Mom's dinner, forty family members were seated at the restaurant as she came strolling in a few minutes later looking beautiful in her two-piece red outfit and tiara. We placed her "90 and Fabulous" sash on the top part of her body. Mom sat at the head of the table. The restaurant provided good service and delicious food. We brought two delightful desserts with us - a cassata cake and chocolate cupcakes. My mother's brief speech ended by reminding us to continue to come together and love each other.

Throughout the dinner, I saw my mother looking around at each of the tables smiling. It was four generations of love. Near the end of the celebration, I asked Mom if she was having a good time. She replied, "This has been one of the best days of my life."

A celebration does not get any better than that.

If you are still at a loss as to how to celebrate, here are a few other examples. Hope, attended several colleges after high school. Like most young people, she was not sure what she wanted to do with her life, but she found a college where she stayed for more than one year. I told her that if, or when she graduated with a four-year degree, I would take her on a trip to the destination of her choice. When Hope graduated with a Bachelor of Arts Degree our family was delighted and she did not forget the promise I made to her several years ago. Four months after her graduation, we spent a week at Disney World.

We went to our local AAA travel agency and purchased a vacation package which included lodging on site, airline tickets, the Disney Dining Plan, 7-day passes, and a pool within a few feet of our hotel room. There was so much to do at this resort. Every day we left out around 9 am and did not return until 9 pm. I marveled at how well organized this amusement park was from our first day until we packed up at the end of the week. My favorite memories were taking a photo of our family by Cinderella's castle and getting a hug from Mickey Mouse.

Saying goodbye to someone you love is never easy, especially if that person has died. Whether the death comes after a long-term illness or unexpectedly, there is so much pain and sorrow to deal with over our lifetimes.

I had the pleasure of meeting Vickie when we both attended the same church 12 years ago. She was quiet, nice, and helpful. Vickie had a good sense of humor and loved her family. The church was very delighted when three of her family members joined the church. Vickie's brother, Ben, was one of the new church members. Ben was tall, cool, and intelligent. Several years after Ben joined the church he was diagnosed with a terminal illness.

He was in good spirits whenever we came to visit him. After Ben died, his funeral was at the church. At the conclusion of the service, Vickie asked all attendees to meet her in the vestibule. She handed each of us an inflated balloon. We took the balloons outside and stood together on the front lawn of the church. We listened as the pastor said a prayer of praise in celebration of the life of Ben. We then released all of the balloons. It was lovely to see all of the balloons gently floating into the air, going in all directions across the sky. It was also a beautiful way to end Ben's funeral service- looking up to heaven hoping that Ben knew how special he was to all of us.

Exercise 7

Today, start to write your list of celebration activities. They do not have to be extravagant or economical activities, but they should be things that give you great joy. Here is a list of suggestions for your consideration:

- Read a book
- Take a walk in the park, your neighborhood or on a beach
- Fly a kite
- Have dinner at one your favorite places or try a new restaurant
- Dance
- Call someone you have not spoken to in several weeks
- Plan a weekend getaway
- Relax on your sofa with your favorite beverage while listening to some good music
- Check out a roller or ice skating rink to see if you still have those moves
- Host a potluck dinner party

- Start a bucket list of places to visit within the next year
- Catch up with a friend at a local coffee shop
- Work on an invention
- Invite people you enjoy being with over for meal and good conversation
- Mail a beautiful card to a loved one expressing your appreciation for all they have done for you
- Buy the ingredients and prepare a new recipe
- Binge-watch one of your favorite series
- Visit a local museum
- Sign up for a sip & paint event
- Stop by an older relative, friend, or neighbor's home with some light refreshments – call first!
- Attend a sporting event
- Volunteer at a local shelter or food bank
- Plan a game night at your house
- Make s'mores in the backyard at the end of your day while stargazing
- Find a place to go horseback riding
- Watch a movie that makes you laugh and feel good
- Enjoy a night out at a concert, comedy club, or theater
- Look through your photos from this year to see all the faces and places that have been a part of your journey and smile

Before you know it, you will be taking a look at that list to decide which activity you will do to celebrate your successful journey.

Author's Note

Thank you for reading this book. I hope that my journey to a contented life will help to guide you as you dare to live a better life, starting today. In closing, I leave you with this prayer:

"May the Lord bless and protect you;
may the Lord's face radiate with joy because of you;
may He be gracious to you, show you His favor
and give you His peace."
Numbers 6:24-26 (TLB)

About Write and Vibe

We are an independent publishing company that believes writers should only have to worry about writing. Meaning, you write your book, we'll do the rest.

To learn more about us, our authors, and their books, please visit us at

Writeandvibe.com | Fb & IG @writeandvibe